ADI'S PERFECT PATTERNS AND LOOPS

written by Caroline Karanja

illustrated by Ben Whitehouse

PICTURE WINDOW BOOKS
a capstone imprint

Meet our coding creatives!

This is Adi. Adi likes arts and crafts. She spends most of her time coloring, playing music, and making things. Whenever she sees something new, she wonders how it came to be. She likes to say, "I wonder . . ."

This is Gabi. Gabi loves to read, play outside, and take care of her dog, Charlie. She is always curious about how things work. Whenever she sees something that needs fixing, she tries to find the best way to improve it. She often says, "What if . . . ?"

Adi and Gabi make a great team!

Gabi is going to Adi's house after school today. When the bus gets to their stop, the girls thank the driver and get off. He waves and drives to his next stop.

Gabi's dog, Charlie, comes up to greet them. "Hello, Charlie!" the girls say.

The mail carrier pulls up in her truck. She is delivering mail to the houses in the neighborhood. "Hello, Ms. Cruz!" the girls call out.

"Hello, girls!" Ms. Cruz says.

"Do you have lots of stops today?" Gabi asks.

"Same stops every day!" Ms. Cruz replies.

"Just like the bus driver!" Adi says.

MAIL CARRIER'S LOOP

PICK UP MAIL

DELIVER MAIL

MOVE TO NEXT HOUSE

"Yep! The bus driver and I make our loops every day—pick up, deliver, repeat!" Ms. Cruz says then hops back in her truck and heads down the street.

"Do you know who else makes loops?" Gabi says to Adi. "Computer programmers! Loops make it so that programmers don't have to repeat commands."

BUS DRIVER'S LOOP

DROP / PICK UP STUDENT

↓

DRIVE TO NEXT STOP

⟳

"Instead of giving the same instructions every time a task has to be repeated, programmers make a code loop that repeats the instructions for them. Then the computer will follow the repeating pattern until the job is finished," Gabi says.

"A bus driver and a mail carrier use loops to perform the same tasks at every stop they make!" Adi adds. "I wonder what other jobs have loops?"

"Lots!" Gabi says. "In factories, restaurants, or offices, lots of jobs run on loops. The same tasks are repeated again and again until the job is done."

What Is a Loop?

In a computer, a loop is a block of code that tells the computer to repeat a task until it's done. Programmers can add statements such as if/then statements in their code loop. For example: If there is a student at the bus stop, then the driver will stop. If there is no student, then the driver will keep going.

Inside the house, Adi sees a large box near the front door. Adi's mom says, "Look what the mail carrier delivered! Grandpa sent it."

Adi opens it and finds a train set. "Wow!" she says. "Want to help me build the track, Gabi?"

"Yes!" Gabi agrees.

The girls take the box to the living room. The train set has track pieces and different types of train cars. It also has some buildings, a remote control, and even some small people.

The girls work on building their track. It has straight parts, curved parts, and bridges.

"Our train has a route, like the bus driver and mail carrier. It also has to repeat tasks at every station," Adi says.

"What if we give the train a code loop to help it do its tasks?" Gabi suggests.

"Great idea! We can make train stations with these," Adi says, holding up one of the buildings. "At each station, the train can run its code loop."

"Now let's make the train," Gabi says.

"Our train is like the block of code," Adi says. "We have to build the code so that it knows what to do at each stop."

"Right!" Gabi agrees. "Our train has three tasks: move to a station, drop things off, and pick things up."

"Things and people!" Adi says.

Patterns

When programmers see a repeating pattern in their code, they create a loop to save time. Instead of having to repeat the same block of code many times in their program, creating a loop will make their program shorter and easier to use.

"OK, let's build our code blocks. First the engine. Its task is to stop the train at each station." Gabi makes a small sign that says *MOVE TO NEXT STATION* and tapes it to the engine.

MOVE TO
NEXT
STATION
↓
DROP OFF
PEOPLE
AND
PACKAGES
↓
PICK UP
PEOPLE
AND
PACKAGES

Adi decides that the blue car's task will be to drop off packages and people that belong at each station. She makes a sign that says *DROP OFF*, and she tapes it to the blue car.

The red car's task will be to pick up packages or people from each station. The girls tape a sign to the red car that says *PICK UP*.

"We've built our code. Should we see how it works?" Adi asks.

"Sure! You can be the computer programmer—like the engineer!" Gabi says. She hands Adi the remote.

"All aboard!" Adi calls out and starts the train.

"*Choo choo!*" the girls say as the train rounds the bend. When it gets to the first station, Adi stops the train. Gabi takes a toy block off the train and leaves it at the station. She puts two people waiting at the station on the train.

"Our code works!" Adi cheers. She gives Gabi a high five.

Gabi says, "Let's run the loop again! *Chugga chugga choo choo!*"

Can you make a code loop?

Adi and Gabi will be selling cookies in their neighborhood. Using a toy or your finger, trace the route they should take to each house. They will have four repeating tasks. What order should the tasks go in? Can you write a code loop for them?

Tasks

GIVE THEM COOKIES

RING DOORBELL

ASK IF THEY WANT COOKIES

TAKE PAYMENT

Glossary

code—one or more rules or commands to be carried out by a computer

command—an instruction that tells the computer to do something; many commands put together make up computer programs

loop—something that happens again and again

pattern—a repeated sequence; things that follow in a specific order

programmer—a person who writes code that can be run by a machine

task—a piece of work that needs to be done

Think in Code!

- What tasks do you do every morning or evening? How does your daily loop start? How does it end?

- Patterns are everywhere. Create a pattern that alternates between different numbers. Try a pattern that alternates between different shapes and colors.

- Write a loop code to use every time you make your favorite sandwich. In what order should the ingredients go on the sandwich? Tape the loop code inside your cupboard for a reminder the next time you make lunch!

About the Author

Caroline Karanja is a developer and designer who is on a mission to increase accessibility and sustainability through technology. She enjoys figuring out how things work and sharing this knowledge with others. She lives in Minneapolis.

This book is dedicated to Noelle for letting me imagine a brighter future
—C. K.

Picture Window Books are published by Capstone,
1710 Roe Crest Drive, North Mankato, Minnesota 56003
www.mycapstone.com

Library of Congress Cataloging-in-Publication data is available on the Library of Congress website.

978-1-5158-3443-4 (paper over board)
978-1-5158-2744-3 (library hardcover)
978-1-5158-2748-1 (paperback)
978-1-5158-2752-8 (eBook PDF)

Summary: Friends Adi and Gabi discover that the coding concepts of repeating loops and patterns are
all around them and have fun making loops of their own with a train set.

Editor: Kristen Mohn
Designer: Kay Fraser
Design Element: Shutterstock/Arcady

Printed and bound in the United States of America.
PA021